Book 1

Name:

Date Started:

Bible Characters Gideon

Name:

Bible Characters

Draw Gideon (and his army)

Read the following scriptures about Gideon:
Judges 6:33;
Judges 7:6, 7, 12, 15, 16, 19-22

Fill in the blank:

Gideon's army defeated the ,________________

the ________________ and the ________________.

____

Ruth was **courageous**. What does this mean?

____

____

True or False (*put correct answer if it is false*)

1. Gideon's army was 3,000,000 men. ___________
2. Gideon gave the men horns and large empty jars with torches inside. ____________
3. The army against Israel was small ___________
4. Gideon told his men to shout "For Jehovah and Gideon!" _______________

Read Judges 7:19-22.
What happened to the army that came against Israel?

Read Judges 6:25-27. Gideon immediately followed Jehovah's instructions and removed the false god Baal.
How can I behave like Gideon and follow directions?

Read James 4:10. **How can I humble like Gideon?**

Gideon called to Jehovah for help and wanted to do his will.
How can I do Jehovah's will like Gideon?
Read Matthew 7:7, 8

Bible Characters Hezekiah

Name:

Draw Hezekiah and/or Jehovah's angel who rescued Judah

Read the following scriptures about Hezekiah:
2 Kings 18:1-36; 19:35, 36; 20:1-6
2 Chronicles 29:10-17
2 Chronicles 32:7, 8

Fill in the blank:

Hezekiah was the King of ____________________

Hezekiah was ___________ years old when he became King.

Soldiers from what country threatened Judah?

____

True or False (*put correct answer if it is false*)

1. Hezekiah was NOT faithful to Jehovah _________
2. Hezekiah's life was miraculously extended by 25 years ______________
3. Hezekiah's father was King Saul ____________
4. Hezekiah repaired God's temple ____________

Bible Characters

What happened to Sennacherib and his army?

Read 2 Kings 18:31, 32. Someone may say something similar about Jehovah to me. **How will I respond? Will I have faith in Jehovah like Hezekiah did?**

Read 2 Kings 18:5, 6. How can I be like Hezekiah?

Hezekiah worked hard to clean up Jehovah's temple. **How can I work hard at the Kingdom Hall?**

Bible Characters 

Bible Characters

Name:

Draw Ruth

Read the following scriptures about Ruth:
Ruth 1:14-18
Ruth 2:11, 12, 17, 18; 4:17, 22
Matthew 1:6, 16

Fill in the blank:

Ruth was supportive to her mother-in-law,_________

Ruth was the ancestor of ________________ and

____

Ruth was **self-sacrificing**. What does this mean?

____

____

True or False (*put correct answer if it is false*)

1. Moab is close to Bethlehem ____________
2. Ruth left her family to go to a foreign land with Naomi ____________
3. Ruth was a hard worker ____________
4. Ruth was lazy ____________

Read Ruth 1:14-18. What happened when Naomi told Ruth to return to her people?	**Read Ruth 4:14, 15**. Having sons was VERY important in Ruth's time, but what did people say about Ruth? **How can I behave like Ruth so Jehovah will be proud?**
Read Ruth 3:11. How can I be like Ruth so that everyone will know that "I am an excellent person"?	Ruth was self-sacrificing and worked hard to care for Naomi. **How can I be self-sacrificing with older brothers and sisters at the Kingdom Hall?**

BIBLE READING MONTHLY SCHEDULE

Month:

Sunday	Monday	Tuesday	Wednesday	Thursday	Friday	Saturday

"I really delight in the law of God."—ROMANS 7:22

How does your life look?	How does your family look?

What are people like?	What are animals like?

What is food like?	What is your favorite thing about the New World?

Name:

Date:

Ministry	Informal Witnessing	Family Worship

Bible Reading	Personal Study	Meeting Attendance

Spiritual Goals

We are blessed to know so many brothers and sisters who have been loyal to Jehovah for many, many years! Reach out to them at the next meeting:

Give a hug to:	
Have an "Interview" with: (using Interview download)	
Go in service with:	
Visit at their home, do yard work or bring a meal to:	

Be like Jesus' father

Name: ______________________________

Date: ______________________________

www.JW-Downloads.com

Joseph

Jehovah had accounts written in the Bible for our benefit!
We will look at Bible Characters and see how I can improve myself by having qualities like them.

Joseph listened to Jehovah's direction	How can I listen to Jehovah's direction like Joseph?
Read Matthew 2:13-15 Jehovah's angel appeared and commanded him to FLEE to Egypt. Flee means to hurry! Joseph knew he had to listen to Jehovah's command because Jesus' life depended on it! Herod wanted to kill him! Joseph and Mary DID NOT QUESTION Jehovah, they immediately got ready to leave.	**When I hear directions from the elders in the congregation, what should I do?** **Even if it seems like what they are saying is not likely, should I still listen and follow directions?** (remember, Joseph and Mary found it hard to believe that someone would want to kill their son, but they listened)

Joseph led a simple life	How can I lead a simple life like Joseph?
Read Matthew 13:55 Joseph worked as a carpenter. This involves hard work and would not make a person rich, but Joseph and Mary were satisfied with this lifestyle. They brought up Jesus as a happy and healthy child and did not lack the things they needed.	**My family provides food and a home for me. These are the MOST important things! Even if others have more than me, should I be content with a simple life like Jesus father, Joseph?** **What are some ways I can make my life simple, so I can have more time for Jehovah?**

Joseph knew the importance of spiritual things	How can I appreciate spiritual things like Joseph?
Read Luke 2:45, 46, 49 Joseph regularly took his family to the synagogue where they learned about Jehovah and his Laws. Jesus appreciated spiritual things very much. Even when Joseph and Mary thought they had lost Jesus, they discovered that he was in the temple, discussing spiritual things with the teachers.	**Does my family appreciate the meetings at the Kingdom Hall like Joseph and his family did?** **Do I take time to ask the elders questions and try to know Jehovah better? How can I improve in this?**

Be Like... Joseph

What Does Your Future Look Like?

Name: Date:

Thanks to Jehovah, we have a wonderful future to look forward to!

Read Revelation 21:4; Psalms 37:10, 11; Daniel 2:44; Galatians 5:22, 23; Titus 1:2

and draw what you see in your future.

Name:

Chapters:

My favorite verse:	Main Idea:

How does it apply today?	What is Jehovah teaching me with these chapters?

Bible Reading Study Guide

Name: Date:

Thankful

I am thankful to Jehovah today because:

I am thankful to my family today because:

Something I can improve on tomorrow is:

Family Worship

Date:________________

Topic for Discussion/Research:

Questions:

Answers:

Interesting Info on this week's topic:

Things I Am Grateful For:

How Can I Help the Friends in the Congregation?

What Can I Do Better?

Spiritual Goals This Week:

DATE: ________________

www.JW-Downloads.com

I Love My Congregation

Choose 8 new congregation members!	
Name: I am thankful for them because: I can help them in this way:	Name: I am thankful for them because: I can help them in this way:
Name: I am thankful for them because: I can help them in this way:	Name: I am thankful for them because: I can help them in this way:
Name: I am thankful for them because: I can help them in this way:	Name: I am thankful for them because: I can help them in this way:
Name: I am thankful for them because: I can help them in this way:	Name: I am thankful for them because: I can help them in this way:

www.JW-Downloads.com

Name:

Activity	M	T	W	Th	F	Sa	Su
Bible Reading							
Ministry							
Christian Life & Ministry							
JW Broadcasting							
Watchtower Study							
Congregation Bible Study							
Family Worship							

My Theocratic Planner

Appreciating Jehovah's CREATION!

Jehovah shows love for mankind through his wonderful works of creation!

Read Romans 1:20 How does our planet show Jehovah's love for me?	***Read Acts 14:17*** How does food show Jehovah's love for me?
Read Genesis 1:24 How does animal creation show Jehovah's love for me?	***Read Psalms 77:11, 12*** How do I show appreciation for Jehovah's creation? How can I increase expressions (and actions) of thankfulness to Jehovah?

Name: Date:

My Goals THIS WEEK

My Goals THIS MONTH

My Goals THIS YEAR

Long Term Goals

My Goals For Jehovah

Family Worship - Memorize Scriptures Part 1
Memory Card Review Page

2 Corinthians 4:16-18

Therefore, we do not give up, but even if the man we are outside is wasting away, certainly the man we are inside is being renewed from day to day. For though the tribulation is momentary and light, it works out for us a glory that is of more and more surpassing greatness and is everlasting; while we keep our eyes, not on the things seen, but on the things unseen. For the things seen are temporary, but the things unseen are everlasting.

Matthew 10:16-18

“Look! I am sending you out as sheep among wolves; so prove yourselves cautious as serpents and yet innocent as doves. Be on your guard against men, for they will hand you over to local courts and they will scourge you in their synagogues. And you will be brought before governors and kings for my sake, for a witness to them and the nations.

Matthew 10:19-22

However, when they hand you over, do not become anxious about how or what you are to speak, for what you are to speak will be given you in that hour; for the ones speaking are not just you, but it is the spirit of your Father that speaks by you. Further, brother will hand brother over to death, and a father his child, and children will rise up against parents and will have them put to death. And you will be hated by all people on account of my name, but the one who has endured to the end will be saved.

Activity Ideas:
1. Print 2 sided memory card game and practice
2. Print the scripture verse on one side and draw a picture on the other side to try and recognize it!
3. Print the scripture name on one side and draw a picture on the other side to try and recognize it!
4. Take turns reading the same scripture aloud
5. All read the same scripture aloud at least 5 times
6. Play charades and act out the scripture
7. Play pictionary, draw the scripture, others guess
7. Give examples on how you can apply this scripture in your life (at work, school, etc)

Matthew 10:28

And do not become fearful of those who kill the body but cannot kill the soul; rather, fear him who can destroy both soul and body in Ge·henʹna.

Matthew 10:37

Whoever has greater affection for father or mother than for me is not worthy of me; and whoever has greater affection for son or daughter than for me is not worthy of me.

1 Peter 3:14

But even if you should suffer for the sake of righteousness, you are happy. However, do not fear what they fear, nor be disturbed.

John 17:14

I have given your word to them, but the world has hated them, because they are no part of the world, just as I am no part of the world.

Romans 8:38, 39

For I am convinced that neither death nor life nor angels nor governments nor things now here nor things to come nor powers nor height nor depth nor any other creation will be able to separate us from God’s love that is in Christ Jesus our Lord.

Matthew 24:14

And this good news of the Kingdom will be preached in all the inhabited earth for a witness to all the nations, and then the end will come.

Psalm 56:11

In God I put my trust; I am not afraid. What can a mere human do to me?

2 Corinthians 4:16-18

Matthew 10:16-18

Matthew 10:19-22

Matthew 10:28

Matthew 10:37

1 Peter 3:14

John 17:14

Psalm 56:11

Matthew 24:14

Romans 8:38

“Look! I am sending you out as sheep among wolves; so prove yourselves cautious as serpents and yet innocent as doves. Be on your guard against men, for they will hand you over to local courts and they will scourge you in their synagogues. And you will be brought before governors and kings for my sake, for a witness to them and the nations.

Therefore, we do not give up, but even if the ma
we are outside is wasting away, certainly the ma
we are inside is being renewed from day to day. Fo
though the tribulation is momentary and light,
works out for us a glory that is of more and mor
surpassing greatness and is everlasting; while w
keep our eyes, not on the things seen, but on th
things unseen. For the things seen are temporary
but the things unseen are everlasting.

And do not become fearful of those who kill the body but cannot kill the soul; rather, fear him who can destroy both soul and body in Ge·henʹna.

However, when they hand you over, do no
become anxious about how or what you are t
speak, for what you are to speak will be give
you in that hour; for the ones speaking are no
just you, but it is the spirit of your Father tha
speaks by you. Further, brother will han
brother over to death, and a father his child
and children will rise up against parents an
will have them put to death. And you will b
hated by all people on account of my name
but the one who has endured to the end will b
saved.

But even if you should suffer for the sake of righteousness, you are happy. However, do not fear what they fear, nor be disturbed.

Whoever has greater affectio
for father or mother than fo
me is not worthy of me; an
whoever has greater affectio
for son or daughter than fo
me is not worthy of me.

In God I put my trust; I am not afraid. What can a mere human do to me?

I have given your word t
them, but the world has hate
them, because they are n
part of the world, just as I a
no part of the world.

For I am convinced that neither death nor life nor angels nor governments nor things now here nor things to come nor powers+ 39 nor height nor depth nor any other creation will be able to separate us from God’s love that is in Christ Jesus our Lord.

And this good news of the
Kingdom will be preached i
all the inhabited earth for a
witness to all the nations, an
then the end will come.

How can I share the following things with the brothers and sisters in my Congregation?

My Time	My Love	My Happiness

My Skills	My Money	My ______________

Happy to Give

Jehovah has FEELINGS

Jehovah has Feelings

Name: Date:

Read Psalms 78:10-17, 40, 41 - How did Jehovah feel about the way the Israelites treated him?	
Is there anything ***I DO IN MY LIFE*** that might hurt Jehovah's feelings?	**What changes can I make?**

Read Proverbs 27:11 - What makes Jehovah happy?	
What do ***I DO IN MY LIFE*** that makes Jehovah happy?	**Can I do more?**

Something (or things) I will improve on/change starting NOW to make Jehovah HAPPY!

My reasons for Joy serving Jehovah!!!

My Reasons for Joy Serving Jehovah!

Name: Date:

Reason #1

Reason #2

Reason #3

JW DOWNLOADS

Bible Reading

Name:

Date:

Bible Reading Guide

Scripture/Verses

Setting: Date/Time

Commentary

Main Character(s)

Other Events/People During This Time

Research (JW.org, publications)

Key Words

COMMANDS, WARNINGS, TRUTHS in this passage

How am I being INSTRUCTED, CORRECTED and ENCOURAGED by this passage?

Apply in My Life

Verse I want to remember/memorize

Daily Bible Reading

Date: ______________________

Scripture	Footnotes

Key People	Key Words

Written to:	Setting, Date
Written by:	Main Theme(s)

Observations

Apply in My Life

Bible Reading Guide

Daily Bible Reading

Bible Reading Guide

Date: ______

Scripture

Footnotes

Key People

Key Words

Written to:

Written by:

Setting, Date

Main Theme(s)

Observations

Apply in My Life

Language:

Language:

Enjoy Hard Work

Enjoy Hard Work

I am excited to work hard at:

(Secular work, work at home, work at Kingdom Hall, work for Those In Need)

I enjoy learning new things because:

(New skills and new trades create new opportunities and expand my knowledge!)

When I work hard, who am I helping? How does that make me feel?

(Family, Friends, Myself...)

I am going to work hard for others by:

(Helping others with their necessities brings great joy from giving!)

A Capable Child

A capable child is TRUSTWORTHY, honest, good

Ways I show I am trustworthy (write a sentence or draw a picture!)

Reference scripture **Galatians 5:22,23**

A Capable Child

Ideas: Show honesty at home and at school. Do not steal.
Show generosity when giving to Jehovah, money or time in service.

A capable child is INDUSTRIOUS, hard working

Ways I show I am industrious (write a sentence or draw a picture!)

Reference scripture **Romans 12:11**

Ideas: Help clean the Kingdom Hall, even if it is not the week that my service group is assigned. Go out in the ministry often.

A capable child EARNS PRAISE

Ways I show I am worthy of praise

(write a sentence or draw a picture!)

Reference scripture Philippians 4:8

A Capable Child

Ideas: Do everything knowing Jehovah is watching. Always make Jehovah and my parents proud with everything I do.

Jehovah is our Refuge

Jehovah is Our Refuge

Name:________________________ Date: ________________________

Define REFUGE: ________________________

____

It is very encouraging to know that Jehovah is our refuge!

Read the following scriptures (check off as you read them)

_____Psalm 34:8

_____Psalm 46:1

_____Psalm 62:8

_____Psalm 91:2

_____Psalm 18:2

_____Proverbs 30:5

_____Joel 3:16

_____Nahum 1:7

How does it feel to have Jehovah as your refuge?

How can I show appreciation for Jehovah's guidance and protection?

Thankful for blessings:

Brothers and Sisters Who Are Persecuted
(from JW.org)

Thankful for:
Health
Happiness
Congregation
Family
Secular Work
Home
Food

Other:

Anxiously Awaiting coming events:

Meaningful Prayers

Date:

Specific Goals I Want to Reach:

Specific Families, Friends who are going through hard times:

My Personal Study

Plot/Setting Summary:

Vocabulary Research

Verse:	Verse:	Verse:	Verse:
Word:	Word:	Word:	Word:
Definition:	Definition:	Definition:	Definition:

People (verse, name, research, new info)

Locations (verse, location, research, new info)

Topics for further exploration

Verse	Footnotes

My Weekly Checklist

Week of:

SPIRITUAL ACTIVITY	M	Tu	W	Th	F	Sa	Su
Daily Bible Reading							
Prayer							
Meeting Attendance							
JW TV (Broadcasting, videos)							
Christian Life and Ministry Meeting Preparation							
God's Kingdom Rules Meeting Preparation							
Watchtower Study Meeting Preparation							
Read Magazines Watchtower, Awake!							
Daily Text							

JW DOWNLOADS

The Shulammite girl was Modest and Humble

Shulammite Girl was Modest & Humble

MODEST: unassuming or moderate in the estimation of one's abilities or achievements.

Ways I can show MODESTY:

Other Bible examples who showed modesty

Proverbs 11:2

HUMBLE: having or showing a modest or low estimate of one's own importance.

Ways I can show HUMILITY:

Other Bible examples who showed humility

Philippians 2:3

Part 1

Was Life Created Workbook FOR KIDS!

INTRO

Name four living things on the cover:

1. ____________________

2. ____________________

3. ____________________

4. ____________________

What is ONE of the questions that this brochure is going to consider?

____

Some people believe creation happened in 24 hour days like we have now and that it happened a few thousand years ago. Others, like atheists, do not believe in God, or in the Bible.

This is what I believe about Creation:

____

____

Hebrews 11:1

I have faith in Jehovah's promises.

"Faith is the assured ______________

of what is ______________ for, the

evident ______________ of

realities that are not ______________."

Page 4: The ______________________ Planet

Everything seems to work perfectly. Our temperature (heat and cold), water cycles, rock cycles, gravity and more! We may go through life and not necessarily notice these things because they all happen naturally and as we expect.

Many would have you believe that all of these are **COINCIDENCES**, that they just happened to occur without intelligent design or Creator.

What do you think? Take a moment and discuss what you appreciate about the earth and the animals and water. Do you think it just happened without a maker?

____

What is the definition of the word COINCIDENCE?

RESEARCH PROJECT: The Water Cycle!

- Go to Google.com and type "The Water Cycle"
- Look for the different parts of The Water Cycle: Evaporation, Condensation, Precipitation, Transpiration, Runoff, Percolation/Infiltration, Seepage. See if you can find more words associated with **The Water Cycle!**

What does each word mean?
What is happening in each phase?

Evaporation

Condensation

Precipitation

Transpiration

Runoff

Seepage

Percolation/Infiltration

OTHER TERMS YOU FOUND RELATED TO THE WATER CYCLE!

•Use the space below to draw a picture of The Water Cycle!

p.5 Write your address:

The **Milky Way** is like the "Country" of your address. The **Solar System** is like the "City" and the **earth's orbit** is like the "Street."

The earth's address is a VERY SPECIAL one and here's why!

The spot where the Solar System is in the Milky Way Galaxy is just right. It has everything we need to live. If the Solar System was too far away, we wouldn't have enough elements to live, but if we were closer, there would be dangers from radiation. We are in the PERFECT spot!

Our earth is also in the PERFECT spot within the Solar System. We are around 93 MILLION MILES from the sun, a location where it's not too hot, or too cold. A little further away from the sun and it would be too cold to support life. A little closer to the sun and everything would die from too much heat!

The sun is also perfect for providing heat energy. It gives just the right amount. It is a very special star!

8

Why is the Solar System's location in the Milky Way Galaxy **so** perfect?

Why is the Earth's location in the Solar System **so** perfect?

If the Earth was any **closer** to the sun, what would happen?

If the Earth was any **farther** from the sun, what would happen?

What do we get from the sun?

What do I know about the Solar System? Google "The Solar System" and learn more! Use the next page to draw all of the planets and the star of the Solar System!

Research Project!

Find 5 new facts about the Solar System or any planet in it and write them below:

1.

2.

3.

4.

5.

Draw the Solar System!

What do you think Earth's "neighbor" is?

Earth's moon is unique! It is about 1/4 the diameter of the earth, making it larger than other moons in the Solar System. Did you know that the presence of the moon is the cause of ocean tides??? The moon also helps the earth stay **spinning** on its' perfect **tilted axis**. Without the moon, the earth would wobble uncontrollably and would not be able to support life.

So what about this ***tilted axis*** and ***spin***? The tilt of the earth causes the seasons! The spinning of the earth is what causes day and night cycles. Plus, the amount of hours in the day and night are perfect. If the spinning was **slower**, the days would be longer and the part of the earth exposed to the sun would get too hot! And the part of the earth away from the sun would get too cold! If the spinning was **faster**, the days would be much shorter and it would cause very high winds that would make life impossible.

How affects does the moon have on the earth?

What would happen **without** the moon?

What affects do the **tilted axis** and the **spin** have on the earth?

JW DOWNLOADS

Earth's Protective Shields!!!

What do you think it is like in outer space? It may seem quiet and dark, but it is **VERY dangerous**! There are meteors flying around and radiation that is very harmful. So how does teh earth stay protected? Inside our home planet there is a core made of **iron**. This causes a **VERY powerful magnetic field that goes way out into space around the earth**. This magnetic field protects the earth from dangerous radiation and solar winds from the sun.

Have you heard of the **Aurora borealis**? These are beautiful flashes of light visible from earth that are caused by solar flares and explosions from the sun.

Search "**aurora borealis**" online and look at the amazing pictures! You may even live where they are visible at night!

What features does the earth have that protect it from the dangers of outer space?

____

____

My research about the Aurora Borealis:

____

EARTH'S atmosphere!

Another feature of protection the earth has is its **atmosphere.** The **atmosphere** is like a blanket that covers the entire earth. It is made of the gases we breathe (like oxygen) but it also **protects** the earth!

There are different layers of the atmosphere. The outermost layer is called the **stratosphere** and it is made of the gas **ozone.** Ozone protects from UV radiation coming from the sun. This allows life to go on with no problems for plants and animals!

This cloud of gases also protects from rocks and boulders that are burned up when they hit the atmosphere. **Without it, the rocks would fall to earth, causing great harm!** When these meteors are burning up in the atmosphere, you can see them! They are often called "falling stars."

Even more amazing, the atmosphere keeps the earth's temperature regulated so the heat does not escape too quickly during the night.

How thankful we are to have such a perfectly designed system of protection for our planet!

PROTECTION!

What is another feature of protection the earth has?

What it is made of?

What is the outermost layer called?

How does the outer layer protect the earth?

What would happen if there was no atmosphere?

What feature(s) of the atmosphere do you like the most?

CYCLES

You've already learned about the water cycle.
Isn't it amazing??! It is absolutely **ESSENTIAL** for life!

Define the word **ESSENTIAL**: ______________________________

____

You and me cannot live more than a couple of days without water. We MUST have it! Our wonderfully designed planet distributes fresh, clean water for our benefit. There are three main stages in the Water Cycle. Let's review them!

1. **Solar power** (power from the sun) **heats water so it is lifted into the atmosphere. This is evaporation.**
2. **Condensation of evaporated water makes clouds!**
3. **Clouds rain, snow or sleet to the ground, (precipitation) ready to be evaporated again!**

What do YOU appreciate about the Water Cycle?

____

____

How do I show my appreciation for the gift of water?

____

Did you know there is a Carbon and Oxygen cycle too?

We breathe in oxygen and breathe out carbon dioxide. With all of the billions of people on the earth, you would think that the oxygen would run out, right?!
Thanks to the Oxygen Cycle, we don't have to worry about that.

The oxygen cycle is done by **photosynthesis**. This is the process of plants taking in carbon dioxide and together with sun energy, makes carbohydrates (food) and oxygen!

Then we take in oxygen and breathe out carbon dioxide for plants to have to make oxygen again! This all happens automatically. How cool!

There is also a NITROGEN Cycle. The nitrogen cycle is necessary for life. Nitrogen makes up about 78% of earth's atmosphere (most of it!). Lightning converts nitrogen into a compound that plants can absorb. Plants then use those compounds when making organic molecules. Then animals eat the plants and get nitrogen. Lastly, when plants and animals die, the nitrogen in them is broken down by bacteria. This releases nitrogen back into the atmosphere and into the soil, starting the cycle over again.

People on the earth make tons of waste, but the earth makes use of everything cycling it all back to be reused again. How does all of this make you feel about the designer and creator of the earth? **How wonderfully it was made!**

What three cycles did you just learn about?

1. ______________________________

2. ______________________________

3. ______________________________

How does the Oxygen Cycle work?

____

What happens in the Nitrogen Cycle?

____

What are the three main steps of the Water Cycle?

____

DISCUSSION:

Do you think the features of the earth show that it had a designer/maker/creator?

If someone said the earth was nothing special, just a product of evolution, how would you respond?

What is most convincing to you that proves the earth was created?

Name all of the reasons you can think of that prove the earth was CREATED!

Research Project!

THE ROCK CYCLE

The Rock Cycle is not mentioned in the brochure, but it is another amazing feature of the earth!

Search "The Rock Cycle" online or at your local library and write down what you learn below: ---See if you can find: The stages (or phases) of the rock cycle, what types of rocks are there?, find a picture and make your own drawing based on it!, how rocks change between types. Go outside and take a look at some rocks! Explore and Learn!!!

For more on the Rock Cycle, search our fellow JW "April Chloe Terrazas" or "Super Science Series" at Amazon.com for SCIENCE BOOKS FOR KIDS!

Part 1 TEST

1. What scripture gives the definition of FAITH?

2. What is a COINCIDENCE? Do you think the earth was formed by coincidence? Why or why not?

3. Name the different parts of the Water Cycle:

4. How is the location of the earth in the solar system such a perfect spot?

5. What would happen if the earth was any closer to the sun?

6. Name 3 planets in the Solar System:

7. What is "earth's neighbor"? And what effects does it have on the earth?

8. What causes the seasons?

9. Why is it important that the earth SPINS?

10. What are the different ways the earth is protected?

11. What are some of the features of the earth's atmosphere?

12. How does the Water Cycle work?

13. Is it possible for the earth to run out of oxygen? Why or why not?

14. What is the name of the process that occurs in plants that turns carbon dioxide into oxygen and food?

Well done! Perhaps say a prayer of gratitude for the wonderful way the earth was made.

Daily Bible Reading

My goal is to read the Bible __________ times each day.

My Bible is easy to see and access

YES NO

If no, put it somewhere you will see it frequently to help you remember!

I will read it -circle your choice(s)

-In the morning
-After school
-Before dinner
-Before bed

Other goals related to Bible Reading:

My prayer to Jehovah to help me keep this goal:

____

____

Field Ministry

My goal is to get at least ____________

hours in the field ministry each month!

What sacrifices can I make to get more time in service each month?

1. ____________
2. ____________
3. ____________

I want to expand my ministry to: (circle)

- -Door-to-Door
- -Cart Witnessing
- -Informal
- -Apartments
- -Letter Writing

Is there any form of preaching that I haven't tried? ____________

What is it? Can I try it this year? ____________

I will try to talk to SOMEONE about Jehovah every day! YES NO

Prayer

Jehovah is my best friend!

How often do I talk to my friends and family? Jehovah is the MOST important! I should talk to him THE MOST!
Can I pray to Jehovah more often that I currently do?
I want to speak to Jehovah at least ___________ times per day!

This year, I want to include the following in my prayers:
Highlight or circle all that you want for your goal!

-Improving my "new personality"
-My family's spiritual health and physical health
-Brothers and sisters who are persecuted around the world (check JW.org for updates)
-Showing all of the "fruits of the spirit" in my life
-Elderly brothers and sisters in my congregation
-The strength to preach with BOLDNESS!
-Show gratitude for everything Jehovah does for me personally
-Ask for forgiveness frequently
-Thankful for the Kingdom
-Daily cares and concerns
-ANYTHING! Jehovah is your friend! He wants to hear anything you want to share!

Meeting Attendance

In Hebrews, Jehovah told us how important the meetings are! We are there to learn, to get encouraged and to encourage others!

My goal is to go to ALL OF THE MEETINGS!

Sign your name on the line   Date you signed

While at the meetings I want to do the following:

(circle the ones you want)

-Comment at least once
-Encourage someone who is having a hard time
-Pay special attention to the elderly brothers and sisters
-Give a complement to someone who gave a talk
-Pay attention, not being easily distracted

What other ways can I do better at the meetings?

Christian Life and Ministry & Watchtower

PREPARATION

Meeting preparation is VERY important and helps me learn as much as possible while at the meeting.

My goal is to prepare for EACH Christian Life and Ministry & Watchtower Study EVERY WEEK!

(The JWDownloads weekly CLAM and weekly Watchtower Guide is very useful!)

Ways I can make my studying even better!

1. Read the entire Bible Reading assignment once out loud, then again to make sure I understand everything happening.
2. Practice the names, listen to recordings online or with the APP to make sure I am saying everything correctly.
3. Look up scriptures listed
4. Plan a prepared comment during the Digging For Spiritual Gems part
5. Ask a parent or a brother/sister in the congregation about a part of the study that I do not understand well. Or just get someone else's ideas about it!
6. Take notes
7. Act out parts of the Bible reading with my family. Get to know the characters and how they were feeling, what they were thinking.

Daily Text

Considering the Daily Text every single day shows how much we appreciate this gift from Jehovah. The Faithful Slave puts together little bits of treasured information for us so we can go out into the world with strength and faith in our God, Jehovah!

My goal is to read the Daily Text EVERY DAY of the YEAR!

Sign your name here Write the date you signed

How can I get the most possible information and encouragement from The Daily Text?

Try some of these options:

-use the Daily Text Activities from @JWDownloads

-Read the verses before and after the Daily Text to understand the situation and who is talking

-Look up the reference article and read about the text, who was speaking, how they felt, what was happening

-Practice reading the text around the verse, working on pronunciation if necessary (using the Bible in the app or online)

-MY IDEA: ______________________

God's Kingdom Rules PREP

Each publication by Jehovah's Organization is a treasure for me! I am going to learn all I can from the God's Kingdom Rules study by preparing in advance EACH WEEK.

Sign name here — Date you signed

Aside from studying the material ahead of the meeting, I am going to do the following to get the most benefit from the God's Kingdom Rules book:
(circle the ones you want as your goal)

1. Read all of the scriptures out loud
2. Listen to Bible verses online or in the app to practice pronunciation
3. Use @JWDownloads God's Kingdom Rules for KIDS Study Guide!
4. Ask questions if I do not understand something
5. Imagine myself in whatever situation is being studied that week
6. Speak about it with my family, setup a play and make props! (Idea for Family Worship)
7. What additional way can I make this study the most enjoyable possible?

Voluntary Donations

Take a moment and view several short videos at JW Broadcasting about our brothers and sisters in congregations around the world. Really **think** about our worldwide unity and love and then consider the following:

How am I blessed by Jehovah? List as many things as you can think of!

____

____

____

Jehovah lovingly let his own son die JUST FOR US! How can I show my appreciation for this with my voluntary donations? Can I increase my donation amount each month? ____________

What type of unnecessary things do I spend money on that could go to supporting the Worldwide work instead?

____

____

My goal is to donate at least $____________ each month to Jehovah. Imagine him smiling as you donate... because you know he is! 😊

Appreciating Creation

How do I show my appreciation for the wonderful creation all around me? Do I show my gratitude by the way I live my life?

My goal is to show GREATER appreciation for amazing creation by: (circle the ones you want)

-Treating animals with kindness and respect

-Doing my part to keep the earth clean

-Saying prayers of gratitude on a daily basis for nature, animals, weather, my abilities as a human

-Taking more time to see nature

-Go on a hikes, walks

-Observe the beauty of nature while preaching

-Volunteer at a local animal shelter

-Recycle when I can

-My idea:______________________________

Reading the Magazines

Just like any publication, our Watchtower and Awake! Magazines are a gift and treasure from Jehovah.

My goal is to read ALL of the Watchtower and Awake! magazines produced by Jehovahs' Witnesses

Sign your name here

Write the date you signed here

Each magazine contains gold, silver and precious stones of information! I want to take in all of that knowledge by doing the following:

(Circle the ones you want for your goals)

-choosing a quiet place to read

-reading slowly so I understand everything I read

-read all of the scriptures provided in the articles

-make notes on stickies and keep the articles in a binder or folder to review my favorite points later

-ask questions

-read the articles MORE than once!

-reading a little bit at a time, all throughout the month

-meditating on the information, putting myself in the situation, increasing my faith in Jehovah, increasing my love of Jehovah

SPIRITUAL GOALS

Month:

Monday	Tuesday	Wednesday	Thursday	Friday	Saturday	Sunday

Daily Bible Reading (color:_______________________)

Daily Text (color:_______________________)

Field Ministry (color:_______________________)

CLAM and Watchtower Preparation (color:_______________________)

God's Kingdom Rules Preparation (color:_______________________)

Reading the Magazines (color:_______________________)

Appreciating Creation (color:_______________________)

Voluntary Donations (color:_______________________)

Meeting Attendance (color:_______________________)

Prayer (color:_______________________)

Read Exodus 3:1-22, 4:1-20, 27-31 and Story 30 in the Bible Stories

The B _ rni _ g B _ _ h

Name: ____________________

Who is the main character?

Where is he located?

Why is he there? Draw a picture:

What is the definition of the word **unusual**?

What UNUSUAL thing was happening?

When he went up to it, what happened? Who was it?

What did Jehovah tell him?

Where did Jehovah want to bring his people?

How did Moses feel about being the one to tell the Israelites?

If someone asked who sent him, what was he supposed to do? And what would he use?

How many miracles did Jehovah give him the power to do? ________

Jehovah told ______________________ to go into the wilderness and meet Moses.

After Aaron told the elders what Jehovah had spoken, what did he do?

____

TRUE OR FALSE:
The people did NOT believe Moses and Aaron.

____

Discussion: How do I respond when Jehovah gives me directions through the meetings, assemblies, conventions and publications? How can I show more appreciation for everything Jehovah gives me? Do I show respect to all of the elders and my family members?

W	P	V	N	O	R	A	A	P	Z
A	N	J	E	H	O	V	A	H	D
W	T	A	G	N	I	N	R	U	B
I	S	R	A	E	L	I	T	E	S
K	C	I	T	S	M	O	S	E	S
O	A	E	L	C	A	R	I	M	V
D	I	R	E	C	T	I	O	N	S
A	T	L	E	P	R	O	S	Y	E

Aaron
Burning
Directions
Israelites
Jehovah
Leprosy
Miracle
Moses
Stick

What I Love About You!

FOR:

What I Love About You!

I love your ____________________

____

You inspire me to ____________________

____

I love hearing about your ____________________

____

I'm humbled by your ____________________

____

I'm grateful that you ____________________

____

What I Love About You!

I love remembering the time we

____

I hope to be as ______________
as you one day.

I love how you always ______________

____

If I were to describe you in 1 word, it would be ______________

I love getting your advice on

____

What I Love About You!

I never get tired of your

____

I love that you encourage me to __________

____

Your ability to __________________
amazes me!

I'd be lost without your ______________

____

I love that you taught me ____________

____

I love how good you are at __________

____

I love to play ______________________________

_________________________ with you.

I love it when you ____________________________

____

It makes me smile when you __________

____

Nobody can _______________________________
like you.

Thank you for ____________________________

____

What I Love About You!

When we are apart, I miss ____________________

__________________________________ the most.

I love going ______________________________________

__________________________________ with you.

You are always right about _________________

____

Your dedication to ___________________________

____________________________ is so wonderful!

You deserve **the award** for _________________

____

Good News From God Activities

Workbook

Name:________________________________

Lesson 1

What is the ___________ ___________

1. *What is the good news from God?*

What does Jehovah want life on earth to be like?

How does Jehovah feel about mankind?

Jeremiah 29:11 "...to give you a

f _ t _ r _ and a h _ _ e."

What have governments controlled by man been able to do about violence, disease and death?

Discuss: What is the "good news" for everyone living on earth now?

What new government is coming?

____

What will life be like for the people in the new government? (UNSCRAMBLE)

PACEE ______________________

OODG ______________________

HLAETH ______________________

Isaiah 25:8 says that Jehovah will wipe

______________ from all faces!

Isaiah 33:24 says that nobody will be

SCIK ______________________

Daniel 2:44 says that Jehovah's Kingdom will do *WHAT* to all the current kingdoms?

2. Why is the good news **urgent**?

Define the word URGENT:

____

____

What has to happen for suffering to end?

____

What conditions *for the time of the end* that are listed in 1 Timothy 3:1-5 do you see happening now?

____

____

____

Discuss: How real is Jehovah's word to me? Do I appreciate how close we are to the end of Satan's system of things?

3. What should we do?

What should I be doing now?

Jehovah's Word is like a letter to me. What is it telling me?

Proverbs 29:25 says that I should not be scared of who?

Why should I NOT be scared?

Discuss: REVIEW all 3 Questions and answer in your own words. Draw a picture sharing the good news with a friend!

QUIZ

What life does Jehovah want for mankind?

Have worldly governments been able to fix violence, disease and death?

What new government is coming?

Describe what the new government will be like:

What WILL NOT HAPPEN with the new government?

What conditions listed at 1 Timothy 3:1-5 are currently happening?

Jehovah's Word the Bible is like what?

Why should I NOT be afraid of man?

Word Search!

T	E	L	B	J	F	X
N	H	N	F	E	T	D
E	T	E	U	H	B	N
M	L	W	T	O	I	E
N	A	S	U	V	B	T
R	E	Z	R	A	L	N
E	H	C	E	H	E	E
V	T	X	A	Z	I	G
O	S	U	S	E	J	R
G	U	E	O	O	P	U
H	G	O	O	D	S	B

Bible
End
Future
Good
Government
Health

Jehovah
Jesus
News
Peace
Urgent

All word searches from Puzzle-Maker.com

Use the following pages to create your own family worship activities!

www.ingramcontent.com/pod-product-compliance
Lightning Source LLC
LaVergne TN
LVHW060640110826
845147LV00018B/1018

* 9 7 8 1 9 4 1 7 7 5 4 5 5 *